6 STEPS

TO SUCCESSFUL MAGAZINE

PUBLISHING

How I Sold 4,000 Magazine Articles & How You Can, Too!

Carolyn Tomlin

About the Front Cover

Magazine writers have a wide area of interest from which to choose. As a freelance writer, you select the topics. In my own writing, I write about the things I know—and often about the things I want to learn. This includes crafts, education, parenting, pets, recipes, and travel.

6 Steps to Successful Magazine Publishing
by Carolyn Tomlin
All rights reserved.
Copyright 2014

Author Website/blog: www.carolyntomlin.com
Book design: The Author's Mentor, www.LittleRoniPublishers.com
Cover Images and Interior Photos Credit: Carolyn Tomlin

ISBN-13:978-1502476166
ISBN-10:1502476169
Also in eBook form

PUBLISHED IN THE UNITED STATES OF AMERICA

6 Steps to Successful Magazine Publishing

How I Published 4,000 Magazine Articles

and How You Can, Too!

Section 1
"Knowing the Magazine; Knowing the Audience"

One mistake that new writers make is a failure to understand the specific magazine they plan to submit articles. With the thousands of magazines on the market, each one is different. Otherwise, there is no reason for its existence.

Another reason for rejection is the writer has not identified the reader or audience. Flip though the pages. Look at the photos of people. Are they teens, young parents or senior adults? Glance at the advertisements. Are they promoting items for men, women, babies or pets?

Section 2
"Generating Article Ideas"

How does a writer come up with ideas? Writing about what you know; writing about what you *want to know* is another way. Writers have a comfort zone. This means the different areas you feel comfortable writing, such as hobbies, travel, family, and others. However, I've discovered that when I write about things I don't know about, I'm educating myself! The reward: an interesting life!

Section 3
"Networking with Editors"

Developing a positive relationship with editors is vital to writing article after article for magazines. Always remain professional and strive to be part of the team. When an editor leaves one magazine and goes to another—stay connected. By following these techniques, you can also write for several magazines within the same company and expand your sales.

Section 4
"Writing a Letter of Introduction & a Query Letter"

Your first means of contact with an editor should be the letter of introduction (trade magazines) or the query letter. This book explains the basic format for each, provides practice, and shows the difference between a query letter that is accepted and one that is rejected.

Section 5
"Outlining and Submitting Your Article"

When writing an article, begin with a plan—or an outline. Who will you interview? Did you find current data on the topic? Will you use sidebars? Bullets? Is your article in a similar format as those in the magazine?
When is it time to let it go and hit "Send?"

Section 6
"Waiting for the Contract and the Check in the Mail"

Hopefully, you'll receive a contract detailing the word count, deadline, rights offered and payment. But what if the article query is rejected? This section offers advice on your next step and how to place the article with another publisher.

Bonus!

As a bonus, I've included Questions & Answers that involve, you the writer. These activities will help you master the information included within these pages. You may choose to answer these questions by yourself, or in a small group.

Dedication

This book is dedicated to my students. From kindergarten through university level, I've seen the spark that comes to their eyes when they discover a moment of truth. In some ways, teaching is a way of living forever. What you share with students, hopefully, they pass on to another. Teaching is a circle without end.

A Personal Note to My Reader

The purpose of this book is to pass on what works for me. These ideas are how I write. They work for me. Between the covers of this book are answers to questions I've been asked over the years.

This workbook is written especially for you—the writer who wants to be successful in publishing for the Christian and secular magazine market. When you attend our all-day writing workshops, we are limited in time and can not cover all the material you need. Corresponding to the workshop title, this book provides a deeper and more advanced study of the chosen topics. Designed to be used at home and when you have time to reflect, this book is a follow up to this seminar. After each section, space is provided for you to interact with the information. Use the additional pages to develop your own ideas by following the examples and format.

Writers can reach millions of readers annually through magazines. Writing not only changes the life of others—it changes your life, also! Our writers are people just like you. Perhaps you've thought of writing for years—but haven't started. Or, if you're like me, I thought no one would want to publish my work. Young people discover that writing can lead to interesting careers. Single parents earn extra money. Stay-at-home Moms and Dads connect with the world while making additional income. Seniors write their memoirs. And others turn an avocation into a vocation. You see, writing has no age limit. There's no retirement until "you" decide it's time to quit. An editor really doesn't care what you look like—or if you stay home and work in your PJs all day, or even if you comb your hair!

I've often said, "When the Lord knows it's best for me over there, in heaven, instead of this earth, I hope someone finds me at my computer with my index finger on the "Send" key of my computer. And that my last manuscript "went" through!

It is my prayer that writing will do for you—what it has done for me. And that you will develop a passion for writing and produce articles and books that make a difference in the lives of others. Let me help you reach these goals.

~With all my best wishes, Carolyn Tomlin

Table of Contents

Introduction 1

Section 1 2

   KNOWING THE MAGAZINE; KNOWING THE AUDIENCE 2

Section 2 17

   GENERATING ARTICLE IDEAS 17

Section 3 21

   NETWORKING WITH EDITORS 21

Section 4 30

   WRITING A LETTER OF INTRODUCTION & A QUERY LETTER 30

Section 5 43

   OUTLINING AND SUBMITTING YOUR ARTICLE 43

Section 6 53

   WAITING FOR THE CONTRACT ...AND CHECK IN THE MAIL 53

Resources 60

Appendices 61

   TIPS FOR BOOSTING YOUR WRITING CAREER IN 10 MINUTES OR LESS 61

Also by Carolyn Tomlin 63

About the Author 67

Seminar Notes 68

Introduction

I wasn't born a writer. In fact, I was in my late 40s when I attended my first writer's conference and starting seeing myself as someone who could write—and enjoy the process. Living in Jackson, TN, I knew of no one who actually wrote and published magazine articles. A friend, knowing that I wanted to write, suggested I attend a local writing group. At last, I could be with others who shared this passion. The meeting was scheduled for 2:00 pm on a Saturday afternoon. Arriving a bit early, I found a chair and waited until the members showed up. One by one, a dozen, or so, came in. At 3:00, someone said, "Well, I guess we should get started." This was followed by at least 30 minutes of sipping tea in dainty China cups. Then, the program consisted of people telling what they had written. Would you believe that "no one" had published! One woman timidly raised her hand and said, "Well, once I wrote a little poem, but I put it in a drawer and no one ever saw it."

Feeling frustrated with wasting my afternoon, I realized that if I wanted to write, I would have to teach myself. This was before we had the Internet on home computers, so I spent hours each week in the library. Searching back copies of *The Writer* and *The Writer's Digest*, I poured over articles of what I needed to know in order to put words on paper. Of those articles that really stood out, I fed endless quarters into the copy machine, took them home and read and reread what other successful writers had to say.

That was years ago. Today, the passion continues to grow and I've published over 4,000 magazine articles and 19 books. Frankly, I've stopped counting the articles, but I sell between 200 and 250 articles annually.

If you're like me and have a passion to write, don't let anyone discourage you. This book will show the step-by-step plan that has worked for me and allowed me to published and sell 4,000, plus articles. Writing can change your life. Doors open. People seek you out. I know of no other career where you can work from home and connect with people all over the world. Another plus: There is no retirement until you choose. Yes, writing is a wonderful life!

Section 1

KNOWING THE MAGAZINE; KNOWING THE AUDIENCE

"We make a living by what we get. We make a life by what we give."

~ Winston Churchill

One mistake that new writers make is a failure to understand the specific magazine they plan to submit articles. With the thousands of magazines on the market, each one is different. Otherwise, there is no reason for its existence.

Another reason for rejection is the writer has not identified the reader or audience. Flip through the pages. Look at the photos of people. Are they teens, young parents or senior adults? Glance at the advertisements. Are they promoting items for men, women, babies or pets?

In a nutshell, this book is about writing and selling magazines articles. The basic steps I teach in writing for the magazine market include:

1. Identify 3 magazines where you want to submit articles.
2. Locate the editor's name, email and contact information at those 5 magazines
3. Identify 3 marketable articles ideas.
4. Identify 2 or 3 sources for interviews—experts in this field.
5. Interview by phone or email these sources.
6. Write a query that includes: the title, headline and lead paragraph. Open with a strong hook that catches the editor quickly.
7. Write the body of the article query.
8. Email your query to the 3 magazines.

The remainder of the book explains in detail these 8 basic steps, plus networking with editors, writing the article outline, and waiting for the check to arrive in the mail.

The first step to writing is to study at least 3 back copies of the magazine for which you plan to submit articles. Most libraries keep these on file. An easier way, search the archives on the magazine's web page. Google the magazine and look under "archives." If this information is not listed on the web page, phone the editorial office for the location.

KNOW YOUR MAGAZINE

The Boot Camp for Christian Writers contains a workshop and books focusing on "The Basic Articles and How to Write Them." These seminars discuss in more detail the different type articles editors need to fill those pages. As you search through magazines, keep in mind the types of articles each magazine publishes. Stay within these bounds when submitting an idea.

In the spaces below, list **3 magazines** that include these type articles, the **contact name or editor,** and the **email**. Check the masthead (found near the front cover and listing addresses, names and emails). If the editor's email isn't listed, look for other staff employees. Is their email listed with first initial, then last name (firstinitial.lastname@nameofmagazine)? Or, is it: (firstname. lastname@nameofmagazine). If you know the editor you can usually hit upon the correct email. Or, a phone call to the general office will provide this information.

Again, by knowing the magazine, writers will be familiar with the type articles each magazine publishes. A quick over-view of each type article follows:

- **How-to Article -**
  A How-to-Article is a step-by-step process of doing something, such as a craft, a recipe, or learning a skill. For example: writing a craft article would begin with a brief description of the craft, a bullet list of material needed, a bullet list of directions for making the craft and close with a word of encouragement that the article

is simple to make and can be shared with others. Include a digital showing the materials used and a digital of the finished product in the query letter.

List three magazines that use "How-to" Articles.

1. Magazine:_____

Contact:_____

Email:_____

2. Magazine:_____

Contact:_____

Email:_____

3. Magazine:_____

Contact:_____

Email:_____

- **Travel Article –**
  Travel articles may include arm chair and actual road trips. Photos are vital to selling a travel article. How can you encourage people to visit a site? How was the food different from your area? Did you provide information on a historic place or event? List special festivals or events in a sidebar. You want the reader to see the area through your eyes. I often include a "What You Need to Know" sidebar that list the contact information, the telephone and website.

List three magazines that use travel articles.

1. Magazine_____

Contact:_____

Email:_____

2. Magazine:_____

Contact:_____

Email:_____

3. Magazine:_____

Contact:_____

Email:_____

- **Personal Experience Article** -
  What have you experienced that can help others? Think of inspirational type articles. Have you dealt with a tragic accident, illness or weather related disaster? Were you terminated from your job? Did the company close down? How did you find funds for your teen's college expenses? Show how you survived and how others can receive hope from your knowledge.

List three magazines that use personal experience articles.

1. Magazine:_____

Contact:_____

Email:_____

2. Magazine:_____

Contact:_____

Email:_____

3. Magazine:_____

Contact:_____

Email:_____

- **Nostalgia Article –**
  Take a trip down memory lane, the good old days. Make the connection between "then" and "now." Revisit your childhood, dating years, the birth of a child, or your first job. Focus on a key-hole effect meaning that you write about only one event in a short article. A nostalgia article shows the past and relates it to life today.

List three magazines that use nostalgia articles.

1. Magazine:_____

Contact:_____

Email:_____

2. Magazine:_____

Contact:_____

Email:_____

3. Magazine:_____

Contact:_____

Email:_____

- **Humor –**
  The focus of the magazine determines the type humor used. For example, if this is a farming or country magazine, the humor needs to relate to the reader. If the magazine is slanted toward educators, humor needs to follow the same audience. How does this magazine use humor? What makes an editor smile? Use yourself as an example: never laugh at another person, an ethnic group or culture. Humor is often found in fillers—that space where editors need a few lines to fill out a page.

List three magazines that use humor-type articles.

1. Magazine:_____

Contact:_____

Email:_____

2. Magazine:_____

Contact:_____

Email:_____

3. Magazine:_____

Contact:_____

Email:_____

- **Newspaper column –**
Includes who, what, when, where and how. Write tight and bright. Edit, then edit some more. Contact newspaper editors and offer the same weekly article in each newspaper by offering First Rights in Your Area of Circulation. This means you will not offer the article to a competing newspaper in the same county or city. Small newspapers may not pay, but you can advertise your books and the workshops you teach. Plus, you develop a following of readers in several cities. Often I'm invited to present a program or give a review of one of my books from a newspaper reader. I've discovered there are ways to be "paid" instead of money as a half-page of advertising could cost hundreds of dollars. Google newspapers in your state. Or, Google each town and search for their newspaper. Daily newspapers usually have a larger budget for freelance as opposed to weekly papers.

List three newspapers you would like to submit articles.

1. Newspaper:_____

Contact:_____

Email:_____

2. Newspaper:_____

Contact:_____

Email:_____

3. Newspaper:_____

Contact:_____

Email:_____

- **Fillers, mini articles and columns—**
  Fillers are used when the word count doesn't complete a column. Also, several magazines use regular features as fillers. Look through the magazine you want to contribute. Are fillers used? If so, send 4 or 5 so the editor will have these available if a column falls short and he needs to fill space. When deadlines are running close, the editor doesn't have time to contact a writer for quick fillers. This technique can lead to assignments for feature articles. With fillers, I submit the short text instead of a query. Write "filler" in the subject line of your email.

List three magazines that use fillers, mini articles and columns

1. Magazine:_____

Contact:_____

Email:_____

2. Magazine:_____

Contact:_____

Email:_____

3. Magazine:_____

Contact: _____

Email:_____

- **Profile –**
Paint a portrait with words, show why this is a special person. How has this person made a difference in the lives of others? Do you have a favorite teacher who made a difference in your life? A World War II veteran who survived a plane crash? Look for people who give back to others. Find ordinary people doing unordinary things.

Does the magazine use groups of people, instead of individuals? For example: "5 Women Who Started a Non-Profit Foundation" or "7 Cancer Survivors Share Their Experience." Know the magazine and understand the type articles used.

List three magazines that use profiles.

1. Magazine:_____

Contact:_____

Email:_____

2. Magazine:_____

Contact:_____

Email:_____

3. Magazine:_____

Contact:_____

Email:_____

- **Devotion—**
  Devotions Include a Bible verse or Scripture reference, illustration that includes a Christian lesson, and prayer. Check the *Christian Writers' Market* for a list of devotion publications. Email and request writer's guidelines. Follow exactly the word count and format. Each denomination publishes a devotion booklet. Know the facts about this denomination or have someone review your article.

List three magazines that use devotions articles.

1. Magazine:_____

Contact:_____

Email:_____

2. Magazine:_____

Contact:_____

Email:_____

3. Magazine:_____

Contact:_____

Email:_____

As you access different magazines, plan your article idea on the type of article the magazine publishes. Don't send a "how-to" article if this type is not used. If a feature article uses sub-topics, include these in your writing. Is the article title a "play-on-words" or specific to the text? As a writer, you want the editor to know you're familiar with the magazine and the type articles they publish. No excuse for not checking. Back issues are on their website.

The *Writers' Market* provides a complete summary of most magazines. I usually purchase this book about every 3 years. Instead of paying full-price, save 75 percent or more when ordering from www.half.com and buy last year's book. Purchase the most inexpensive edition. Most of the information is still relevant, but check with the editorial office for the present contact person. Some publications do not respond to the editors of this research book. Google the magazine to find current information.

In additional to magazines listed in *The Writer's Market,* there are numerous publications unlisted. Serious writers are always on the lookout for new opportunities.

One of my most profitable markets comes from an agricultural magazine I noticed at my insurance office. When I checked, I found they publish eight monthly magazines, with a north, south, east, and west edition. That makes 32 magazines! If I could write for one, I could write for several.

KNOWING THE AUDIENCE

Knowing the "magazine" and knowing the "reader or audience" are important in writing-to-publish. Who advertises? Is this a professional magazine that reaches a select group? Is the reader part of the Christian music industry, food service, or a classroom teacher?

How to Identify Your Audience

Like a speaker who lectures or teaches a group of people, knowing those to whom you speak is important. For example, if your audience consists of parents of preschool children, you wouldn't speak on teenage drivers. Or, if your audience consists of insurance agents, you wouldn't teach a class on good nutrition for healthy living.

Match your audience (readers) to the topic you write. How can a writer know the reader? Identify the reader by studying the magazine. Check at least 3 months back copies or the online archives.

Who Are the Readers?

By studying the magazine, you'll see articles, photos and advertisements that describe your reader. For example:

- **Social and economic level.** Do the photos show luxury cars and expensive homes? Or, is there an article on budget travel?

- **Education.** Do articles focus on careers that require professional training? Or, are people learning from life experiences and volunteer opportunities?

- **Leisure Activities.** Does the article promote international travel or cruise ships with luxury accommodations? Or, do photos and articles focus on budget activities such as camping or "10 Ways to Serve Hamburger"?

- **Professional and Careers.** Is this a trade journal provided to a group within this profession? Trade journals depend on advertisements from the field they promote. This pays the cost of the magazine as it is not sold in bookstores. The publication is mailed to individual policy holders or customers.

- **Male/Female.** Does the article focus on issues for "only women" or "only men"? Do you see photos of teenage boys, or girls?

- **Age.** Both the articles and photos will clue you to the reader's age. Are there ads for playground equipment? Or, are there ads for elder use? Look at the titles of articles. Do you see one on "5 Ways Grandparents Can Connect with Grandchildren?" You know this is a magazine for senior adults. But if an article states: "5 Activities Children Enjoy with Grandparents," this is written for children. Double your sales and make your research time count. How? Write the article for grandparents and tweak it for a children's magazine.

Choose a magazine where you would like to submit an article. Check the *Writers' Market* and online archives. Using the topics above, look at the photos and advertisements to find the answers to these questions:

Name of Magazine_____

1. Identify the social and economic level:

_____

2. Education level:

_____

3. Leisure activities:

_____

4. Professional or career:

_____

5. Male/Female Focus:

_____

6. Age:

_____

After you've identified the reader, break it down into sub-topics. For example:

Parents (General) –Budgets, child care, leisure time, other

_____

Parents of Babies –teething, potty training, sleep patterns, other

_____

Children – Making friends, pets, school, sports, other

_____

Teens – Dating, driving, technology, other

_____

Seniors – Health care, retirement, travel, other

_____

QUESTIONS FROM WRITERS—ANSWERS YOU NEED

Q.-1. Can you take one type of magazine article and turn it into another for a different magazine?

A-1. Yes, but change the interviews, quotes, and slant of the article. For example, you've written a "How-to" article on turning trash into treasure. Write an "Interview" article on someone who does this as a hobby. Where do they find the throw-aways? What is his advice for helping others turn their backyard into a Folk Garden?

15

Q-2. What is a good method for researching one idea and generating numerous articles?

A-2. Let's face it! Research takes time. So, to get the most miles from your work, this works for me. I look at a topic, such as "Dogs" and visualize a wagon wheel with the hub as "Dogs" and each spoke another topic. I could list breeds of dogs, dogs raised as guard, companion, work, or child friendly. Another spoke could list medical issues. Another traveling with your dog, or hotels that were 'pet friendly'. Another spoke might list buying from a breeder or adopting a shelter dog. You get the gist—there is no limit on the number of articles that can come from the basic idea. Grab a pen and paper and get started! One day, when your well runs dry, you'll have a list of topics from which to choose.

3. Q-3. What is the quickest way to determine the audience of a magazine?

A-3. Spend a few minutes in the magazine section of a bookstore. Scan through several magazines and look at the photos. Look at the age of the people, the gender, the type of vacations they take and the food they eat. You'll have a somewhat clearer profile of your readers—the audience who will read your article.

Section 2

GENERATING ARTICLE IDEAS
Writing What You Know; Writing What You Want to Know

"Take up one idea. Make that one idea your life - think of it, dream of it, live on that idea. Let the brain, muscles, nerves, every part of your body, be full of that idea, and just leave every other idea alone. This is the way to success."

~ Swami Vivekanana

"I've come to believe that all my past failure and frustrations were actually laying the foundation for the understandings that have created the new level of living I now enjoy."

~Tony Robbins

How does a writer come up with ideas? Writing about what you know; writing about what you *want to know* is another way. Writers have a comfort zone. This means the different areas you feel comfortable writing, such as hobbies, travel, family, or others. However, I've discovered that when I write about things I don't know about, I'm educating myself! The reward: an interesting life!

An agent once told me to focus on one topic—to be known as the writer who wrote about a particular subject. Perhaps that was good advice; but can you imagine how boring life would be if I only used "one" topic for the 4,000 magazine articles I've published? Not all advice is good!

MAKING YOUR ARTICLE IDEAS WORK

Students often pitch good idea—but they're not working. Few markets exist for their ideas. For example, only a few magazines exist for parents of teens and grandparents.

I've had students say they want to write, as an example, on nutrition. Well, "what" about nutrition? Do they mean selecting the right foods, buying organic, balancing the food pyramid, or healthy cooking? Nutrition is a book—not an article. Ideas are great but a writer needs more to flesh out the article.

You have two strategies when pitching an idea to an editor. First, let's say you have a great idea, so you write up the article and try to match it with a magazine. Or second, you study back copies of the magazine, identify the reader or audience, and write your article in the format already used by the publication. Either, will work. But for me, I prefer the second option. Why? You can spend hours or days searching for a magazine where your article fits. I save time by going with the second option of writing to a specific magazine.

Develop a practice of brainstorming ideas. Some are duds and weeded out quickly. Others deserve consideration. Serious magazine writers spend time reviewing publications. Locate magazines not found in book stores or on the magazine isle of your grocery. Check for those outside your usual area of knowledge or skill. For example, read trade journals. Read, read and read some more! If you expect your writing to focus on magazines—read magazines!

If you have an idea for an article you just have to write, check out the newsstands. Look in *Writer's Market* or Google your topic plus the name of the magazine. Post on social media and ask your friends to help find a market.

If you're unable to find a good match, make changes so the article works for another market.

DEVELOP A PASSION FOR MAGAZINES

In order to generate article ideas, develop a love for magazines. An editor will know if you're unfamiliar with her publication. Why? The pitch is off-the-wall and far removed from the intended audience.

One of the tools of the trade is magazines in your area of expertise. Yet, many writers expect to be published without having a background in this medium. For example, if you're a carpenter, would you expect to work without a hammer, saw, lumber, or other necessary equipment? Or, if you interviewed for a job as a gardener, would you tell the interviewer that getting your hands dirty was the pits. Freelance writers need knowledge of the materials from which to earn a living.

If you consider yourself a serious freelance writer, it's work! And if you expect to have your name in the big markets, you need to know the magazines.

So, the next question is: How do I find these magazines—on the cheap? This works for me: Ask those offices you visit to save you back copies. About once a month, I call the vet's office, my doctor, dentist, insurance—anywhere I've seen magazines. I offer to take them off their hands so "they" won't have to haul them out to the trash pickup. Develop a good relationship with the office staff and they'll start saving these for you. Simply, drive by monthly and pick up your treasures. And if these plans fail, shell out and buy them!

For today, read a magazine from cover to cover. Look at the photos, advertisements, articles—everything. Make a list of the ideas that come to mind. Of course, you can't keep them all. Of those I want to save, I store in a six-drawer plastic storage bin in alphabetical order. And yes, you "do" have to purge often. Or else, they will devour your home. Once I dreamed the magazines had taken life and driven me out of my house! Really!

QUESTIONS FROM WRITERS—ANSWERS YOU NEED

Q-1. Some days I just don't want to write. Ideas just won't come. Any suggestions?

A-1. Let's face it; there are just some days that aren't meant for writing. If this happens to you, don't fight it. Walk the dog, call a friend for lunch, read the *Writer's Market* and list those top paying markets. (When I purchase a new Writer's Market, I look for magazines with the symbol $$$ or $$$$). Give yourself a few hours to recharge your batteries. Jot down the time you will return to your work and honor this commitment.

Q-2. My problem is having too many ideas and I can't narrow them down or group them into categories?

A-2. Consider yourself blessed! I suggest you keep a journal listing every time you come up with a saleable idea. Flesh it out immediately so you won't forget the specifics. (Meaning, add data, research, who you will interview, and time-sensitive material). Don't become one of those writers who has hundreds, or even thousands, of profitable thoughts but they've never moved beyond the "idea" stage. Place it on your calendar as to when you'll work on that particular topic.

Q-3. What if I have a great idea and see my idea used in another magazine?

A-3. There is nothing new under the sun. Narrow your idea, come up with another slant, use other sources and interviews and still make it your own. Or email the editor, mentioning the idea and say: "I read with interest the XYZ article. Have you thought of publishing a follow-up article on this topic?" Or take a different slant on the same topic? The editor is pleased to have a positive response to another contributor and you have a chance of writing another article on the subject.

Section 3

NETWORKING WITH EDITORS

"The key to success in life is using the good thoughts of wise people."

~ Leo Tolstoy

Webster's Dictionary defines "networking" as using a set of connections, arrangements, associations, a group, or a set of contacts. Synonyms include meeting people, making contacts, exchanging ideas, and interacting with others. Writers would do well to remember this definition! In my opinion, networking is one of the most important factors in reaching multiple markets. One satisfied editor tells another publication about your professional work. Or, if several magazines are published by the same company, editors talk about writers around the water cooler. What will they say about "you" as a writer? Hopefully, they'll share words like the following:

- This is one writer who always meets our deadline.
- If a change is needed, I know she will respond within 24 hours.
- If I have to reject an article—it's no big deal!
- When I need a new idea on an old topic, I can depend on this writer for a fresh start.

Or, does the editor share these statements about your work?

- We covered this topic six months ago. Didn't the writer check back issues?
- I've save space for this contracted article. The deadline passed two weeks ago. I wonder if the writer plans to send the article?
- I hate to reject this article... again. But it doesn't meet the needs of our magazine or our readers.
- This manuscript was addressed to an editor that left our company a year ago.

12 TIPS FOR WORKING WITH AN EDITOR

Who are the writers an editor comes to again and again with an assignment? Those they can work with. And those who work in a proficient way. These suggestions will help you become the writer editors need.

1. **Deal with Rejection in a Professional Manner**. If an editor takes time to write a personal note, such as "Try us again." Or, send more ideas!" take this as a personal response. Follow up immediately while your name is still fresh with the editor. And, thank her for responding to your email. Then, send out another query—making it the best possible. Within hours!

2. **Don't 'haunt' the Editor or Become a Pest**. If you receive a rejection, get over it! Learn from the rejection and make changes to a new query letter. Never confront the editor as to changing his mind.

3. **Don't Appear Desperate When Contacting an Editor.** Keep your personal life separate from your professional life. Never beg or bargain for the editor to use your work.

4. **Get it Right!** This means knowing the correct name for the editor and the gender -- male or female? Don't rely on spell-check as you may miss some spellings. Proof read your letter before submitting.

5. **Stay in Touch.** What if an editor says he will present your query at the next committee meeting? If you haven't heard from him in two weeks or a month, email or call. Copy the query to the fresh email. Offer to send more queries. This has worked for me in receiving new assignments.

6. **Stay Aware of Trends in Your Field.** "New" sells! If you come across new data, a recent book or trends in your field that an editor would have interest in, share these with the person. Send to editors you've worked with and those you want to write for.

7. **Dealing with Deadlines.** What if sources your editor suggested haven't returned your calls? Notify the editor and ask for others. Emergencies and illnesses happen. Contact the editor as soon as possible and ask for an extra day or two. Do this as early as possible—as editors have deadlines, also.

8. **How do I keep tract of deadlines?** I write the date on my calendar two weeks early. If at all possible, this is the time I honor. However, I know there is a cushion of time if emergencies occur. For some reason I can't understand, I've always enjoyed marking through a completed assignment/deadline with a red pen!

9. **While Writing.** Editors like to know a writer is working on the assignment and will meet the deadline. Email good news, such as a completed interview, new data or digitals ready-to-go.

10. **Continue to Communicate.** After the article is published, write a 'thank-you' note to the editor. Make a positive comment on the format of the published article. Continue building a professional relationship.

11. **Keep Your Information Current.** Every two or three months, send an update of your writing and ask if there is anything you can produce for their magazine. Don't forget to update emails or other contact information.

12. **Social Media Protocol.** Most editors are okay with using Twitter for contacts, but Facebook is for personal information. It's all right to follow the magazine itself. Adding links to published articles on my web page, I can easily communicate with editors. A link doesn't bog down their email and they have a choice or reading, or not. A webpage puts you in control. Post those that are a good example of your work.

13. **Other ways to network.** Birthday and Christmas cards are inexpensive, yet remind the editor you are thinking of them. While visiting an editor, I noticed several Christmas cards taped to her door. If your editor receives a promotion—why not send a small gift card? Some companies have a limit on what employees can receive. The bottom line—editors are your friends. Everyone likes to be remembered![1]

Think about this: How can you begin to build a solid-working relationship with editors? Are there additional ideas of networking which could work for you? List them here:

1. _____

2. _____

3. _____

---

[1] Some information adapted from "How to Build a Relationship with an Editor" Monday Motivation for Writers, from The Renegade Writer

CHOOSE THOSE YOU WRITE FOR

One of the benefits of being a freelance writer is you can choose the people you work with. What if an editor is difficult to work with, requires a half-dozen rewrites, neglects to send contracts, and pays pennies? The next time she contacts you about an assignment, be too busy. Yet, stay professional. And the next time, you'll still *too* busy. And continue to be *too* busy.

Once an editor found one typo in a 2,000-word article she assigned. She climbed on her soap-box and berated me for one mistake. Perfection doesn't exist! It's human nature to respond to such a put-down, but instead of answering and adding more fuel to the fire, I marked her off as a person I didn't want to work with, again. Amen! And Amen!

DEVELOP A UNIQUE SLANT

What skills or work ability do you have to offer? Can you write "tight and bright"? Can you produce a saleable article in a short period of time? Do you have a list of sources readily available? Can you produce top digitals and present them as a package deal? Hone these skills that make you unique and use them as a marketing tool with editors. You'll be surprised how many editors have pages to fill when another writer didn't meet the article deadline.

Developing a unique slant is a strong point in networking with editors.

NETWORK BY ASKING FOR MORE MONEY

New writers often make the mistake of being so grateful for assignments, they'll work for pennies. When I first started writing magazine articles, I was more interested in collecting published clips. Plus, I often wrote for free, against the advice of experienced writers. (The following section explains how you can profit from free work.) If you've written for a magazine several times and continue to receive the same fee, ask for an increase. Try doubling the amount offered. For example, if offered $200, say you were thinking of more like $400. If he says, "Would you accept $300?" Say, "Yes, I enjoy writing for you. So, sure, I'll accept that amount!" In just a few minutes, you've increased your fee by $100.

Sometimes this works—sometimes it doesn't. But I've never felt I harmed the relationship by asking. My philosophy: They can always say "No". I've found that certain columns and departments have a specific budget and editors can not make a change. Maintain goodwill and conduct yourself in a professional manner. Remember, as a freelance writer, you're in charge. You can choose those market for which to write.

WRITE IN EXCHANGE FOR PUBLICITY

Often the small weekly newspapers are hanging on by their teeth and can not pay an honorarium. However by writing for these weekly newspapers, I'm able to promote my books and writing-to-publish workshops in the byline. Did you know a half-page ad in a newspaper can cost hundreds and even thousands of dollars? There is more than one way to be paid—sometimes it's an exchange of work for your personal promotion. The old barter system is still alive and well!

If I submit a reprint to six weekly newspapers with each averaging 5,000 subscribers each week, I've marketed my books and workshops to 30,000 readers. Isn't this more important than the small honorarium the paper is able to pay?

I try to sell only First North American Serial Rights when possible. After the article is published, the magazine/newspaper still owns the article and they can use it in other publications. Some require 3 months after publication; others 6 months. This is where reprints are valuable. I encourage writers to develop several areas of interests. As opportunities arise, pull from your published clips and sell or allow a small publication to use them in exchange for promoting your books or the workshops you teach.

A writer's bio introduces you to an editor or publishing house. Don't be shy—write about your accomplishments! Write in third person and make your bio sparkle! On yes, stay within the one-page limit. Reduce the size type if needed.

Writer's Bio
Carolyn Tomlin
Street Address
City, State, Zip
Email: tomlinm@bellsouth.net
Web page: www.carolyntomlin.com

Carolyn Tomlin has been in the field of education for over 33 years. During this time she was the director of a preschool program, a kindergarten and elementary teacher, Assistant Professor of Education at Union University, and retired in 2001 as the grant writer for the Jackson-Madison County School System. In four years she raised over $5.5 million dollars.

Tomlin has combined her educational career with that of writing and photography. Since 1988 she has published 19 books and over 4,000 articles in the secular and Christian magazines, including: Journal Communications, Inc. (Bowling Green, KY; Jackson, TN Magazine, Images of Bartlett, TN, Asheville, NC, Dickson, TN), *American Profile, Entrepreneur, Bus Tours Magazine, Sunbelt Restaurant Magazine, PTO Today, Today's School, Growing Edge, Tennessee Magazine, Tennessee Home and Farm, GRIT, Early Childhood News, The Kansas City Star* Newspaper, *Woodall Travel Magazines, Mature Living* and others. The award winning book, *The Secret Holocaust Diaries: The Untold Story of Nonna Bannister* (Tyndale) was published in April 2009 with co-author, Denise George. Recent books include: *What I Wish I'd Known Sooner: Parents* and *Teachers* and six books on writing available as an eBook and printed edition with Amazon.com. and Barnes & Noble.

As a regular monthly columnist, she writes the Senior column for *Living Light News* (Canada); "A Parent Speaks" for *The Baptist &*

Reflector, "The Best of the Rest" for *Mature Living* and the "Home & School Connection" a weekly column for several newspapers.

Tomlin is a frequent speaker for teacher/parent workshops and teaches writing conferences. During the 1990s she was an annual speaker or workshop leader for LifeWay Writers Workshop in Nashville in which she encouraged others to become published authors. As the co-owner of "Boot Camp for Christian Writers," she teaches seminars on writing-to-publish at Beeson Divinity School at Samford University in Birmingham and other universities. A frequent speaker at universities, civic clubs, women's Christian groups and libraries, Tomlin combines travel writing while teaching workshops in China, Russia, and the Caribbean,

Tomlin received a B.A. in Elementary Education from Union University, Jackson, TN; a M.Ed. in Elementary Education with a concentration in Early Childhood Ed, a certification in Supervision and Administration from the University of Memphis and has completed all course work for the Doctor of Education Degree.

She is a native of Jackson, Tennessee where she lives with her husband, Dr. Matt Tomlin. They are members of First Baptist Church, Jackson. The couple has two adult children and six grandchildren. A shelter dog, Ernest Miller Hemingway, shares his life with the family.

WHO ARE YOU?

If you're like me, I'm often asked, "What do you do?" Well, if I'm in a group of professional people, I usually say, "I'm a writer and a retired teacher." Although this usually answers their question, I started thinking about my response. So, now it depends on the group. Are they gardeners, or parents of teens, or grandparents? Do they own their own business, or teach school, or sell automobiles? Are they potential writers who might attend one of my workshops? Use this as an opportunity to promote your work.

Now I say, "I'm a freelance writer specializing in travel, gardening, parenting, education and crafts articles. I write for national and regional magazines and teach writing-to-publish workshops."

Have a ready answer when asked. Your "Who Are You?" speech may change—depending on who asks. Oh yes, that gives me the opportunity to hand the person a business card—which I always have ready. Order business cards at www.vista.com. The first 250 are free.

QUESTIONS FROM WRITERS—ANSWERS YOU NEED

Q.1. What can you do, that other writers can't?

A.1. Let's face it: The competition is stiff! My advice: Find something you can do—and do well—that others writers can't or won't do. Let's be honest: Are you good at cranking out saleable article in a hurry? Do you have links for excellent sources for interviews? Can you speak a second language? Often the difference between writers that obtain contracts and those who don't is to become indispensible to a magazine.

Q.2. What is the best approach to respond to a rejection letter?

A.2 If this is the first time to pitch to this editor, think of it as a way to build a relationship. Email a warm and polite "thank-you" note for reviewing your email. While your name is still on the editor's mind, pitch another idea. Each time, write the best query letter possible. This process may take several tries, but eventually, you'll receive that contract—if you know the magazine and know the audience.

Q.3. A student says, "I've developed a positive relationship with an editor. She has given me numerous contracts. Now, she is leaving. What should I do?

A.3. Is she moving to another publication? If so, follow her. Who is taking her place? Write a letter of introduction and several pitches. If the magazine has used you before, they are likely to continue to need your work.

Section 4

WRITING A LETTER OF INTRODUCTION & A QUERY LETTER

"You only get one chance to make a first impression."

~ Author Unknown

Your first means of contact with an editor should be the Letter Of Introduction (LOI) for trade magazines and/or the query letter. This section explains the basic format for each, provides practice, and shows the difference between a query letter that is accepted and one that is rejected.

WRITING A GREAT QUERY

If you want to make time count, first write a Letter of Introduction (LOI) for (trade magazines) and a query for other magazines. Follow this advice before spending hours on a manuscript that may never be read. These letters introduce you to the editor. What should you do if you have a great article idea? First study the magazine and know the audience as stated in Chapter 1. Is this idea a good match for the publication? If the answer is "yes," write a query letter to the editor. First, the query letter should grab the editor's attention. Second, it should make you look like a professional writer. And third, it should sell your idea. However, there's more to making a sale. Look at this guide for creating a query letter that should give you a contract.

1. **Check for the right editor.** Often a magazine will have different editors for each department. Make sure you have the right one. If the name doesn't give a clue as to the gender, call the 800 number and ask if the editor is a Ms. or a Mr.

2. **Begin with a hook.** It's been said that editors only read the first or second sentence of a query. That means, you must grab them fast and keep their attention. Easy? Yes, if you know how to start. Begin with a statistics such as: Two-thirds of adults in the U.S. are overweight, yet they aren't aware of future health issues this problem causes." This is much more interesting than you telling the editor that you've published over 100 articles or that you have a degree in journalism. This should come later in the one-page query.

3. **My best advice: Check the magazine**. What hook do other writers use? Anecdote, quote, or data? Start your query the same.

4. **Show why this topic would have merit for this magazine.** Would readers be interested in this topic? Mention recent news reports or media attention that would make this a priority article. Is there a new book out on the topic? Find these new ideas in your local and national newspaper, as well as TV news programs. Mention the subject is "time-sensitive" in the query. Meaning, if it's NEWS, you need to submit the idea elsewhere if they aren't interested—quick! Give them a couple of weeks. If you haven't heard, email again or call the editor. If you don't have a contract coming, move on to another magazine.

5. **Give a brief outline of the main points of your article.** Mention any interviews, personal experience, other data or statistics to include. Will digitals photos be included? A rule of thumb is 300 DPI (dots per inch) which will give a clear focus for a front cover, if needed. Acceptance improves when you can present a package (manuscript and photos). If a magazine has the expense of sending a photographer to the site, this means additional costs. Say the company is located in small town—would they "really" send a

photographer to China to make a couple of photos of The Great Wall? If you, the writer, can supply the digitals, you are ahead of the pack.

6. **Sell yourself**. Why are you the best writer for this assignment? For example: Have you been obese and lost a great deal of weight? Have you worked with people who had health-problems due to obesity? Mention published clips on this topic if available. If not, mention volunteer work you've done related to weight gain or healthy living.

7. **Ask permission to send article.** I usually write, "May I submit this (article title and word count) for XYZ magazine?"

8. **Close by thanking the editor for reviewing your query**. Such as, "Thank you for reviewing this query. I look forward to hearing from you."

I see two ways to write a query letter and it depends on the tone of the magazine. One, use a professional style, like a business letter, to the point, without being cute. Use letterhead or center your name and address on the top. Use the correct editor, and the full address. In the first style, I address the query to Dear Mr._____ or Dear Ms._____. If they respond in an email or SASE (Self-addressed typed enveloped) and use their first name, this indicates its okay to use it with the next correspondence. Single space with double spaces between paragraphs. A few magazines request the entire manuscript; most request a query. Use caution on those that request a manuscript, as they may not pay. A contract states your honorarium, deadline and rights you are selling. You need this!

A second approach to writing a query letter is less formal. After researching the tone of the magazine, I follow a similar style with a query letter. A name doesn't indicate age, but now I usually use a first name on the query. I've never had an editor correct me for this greeting. If the magazine uses humor and a light approach, do the same.

Check the writer's guidelines for the preferred method of delivery. Today, most editors will accept an electronic query, but some still request a hardcopy and self-addressed stamped envelope (SASE). Provide links to published articles. If you include a hardcopy of published clips, place this package in an 8"x10" mailing envelope. You can send 5 sheets of copy paper for one first-class stamp. If you're unsure, weigh at the Post Office. If the magazine is located outside the United States purchase return International postage. Never send a package with "postage due." I save money on the returned manuscript by stating in the cover letter that a self-addressed post card is included for their response. Do not return the published clips or manuscript. Fortunately, most editors prefer to correspond through email. For those that request regular mail, I've called the editorial office and asked about sending a query by email. So far, this has been acceptable.

A PITCH: TO SEND OR NOT TO SEND?

I think of a pitch as a shorter version of a query. Yet, to some editors, they are one and the same. Sometime writers will not send to XYZ magazine because they fear the risk of rejection. You have a great idea, but lack the confidence to move forward. Allow the editor to be the person who rejects your query—not you. Therefore, don't' reject yourself before the editor has a chance to look over your idea. Too often, we are our own worst enemy.

Writing is personal. Writers face more rejection by throwing ideas out to an editor. But look what you lose by not trying! Even a rejection letter can be seen as a way to connect. The editor may respond by a negative response letter, but she may also offer some advice that can lead to an assignment later. Such as:

- Accepts your idea and gives you an immediate assignment. (Way to go!!!)

- Says, "We appreciate all the time you've put into this idea. However, it doesn't meet our needs at the present. Please try us again!" (This is what I consider a *negative-positive response*. Write a brief thank-you email for reviewing the pitch. Then, in a matter of hours, send in another idea. Make it the best possible by knowing the magazine and the readers.)

- Suggest you make changes to your query and rewrite. (Sounds interested!) Do this within 24 hours.

- Rejects your thoughts but would like to keep your name available for future articles. (Wow! Stay in touch!)

- No response. You email a second time. Still no response. Move on to another market. There are thousands of others that need you!

Remember, it often takes several queries with the top-paying markets to receive an acceptance from a query letter. Don't give up! Winston Churchill said, "All we have to fear, is fear itself." If you wondering about submitting a pitch, go ahead. What is the worst thing that could happen? Will the sky fall? Will you lose your home? They could say "No", but they may say "Yes" and you're on your way to working with a new market.

EXAMPLE OF A GOOD MAGAZINE QUERY

Carolyn Tomlin
Street address
City,State, Zip
Email: tomlinm@bellsouth.net

Date_____

Editor's correct name
Magazine
Address

Dear (editor's name)
Article title: Teen Smoking: Can Parents Make a Difference?
A new report states that approximately 440,000 Americans die each year from diseases related to smoking. About 90% or 396,000 of all cigarette users started as teen smokers. (www.teenhelp.com)

I would like to propose an article for title of magazine that gives parents steps to avoiding or correcting the stated problem. The Center of Disease Control states that, "Regular smoking decreases significantly with an increase in the number of sports played." Being active in sports shows a marked decrease in tobacco use.

Knowledge is power. The article will encourage parents to talk to their teen about the dangers of smoking. When he/she is offered a cigarette, he will have the answer. I'll interview (name of doctor), a parent of a teenager, and a social worker who personally sees the health consequences of teens using tobacco.

I have a personal interest in teaching teens to avoid all forms of tobacco. My father was a heavy smoker who died of lung cancer. Whenever we took a car trip, smoke filled the automobile. And yes, he started smoking as a 16-year-old. When he was diagnosed with cancer, he said, "I would give anything I own--to have never started smoking."

(Editor's name), may I submit "Teen Smoking: Can Parents Make a Difference" a 1,500-word article as a feature/photo package for (name of magazine)? If only one family could avoid this tobacco addiction, the article has made a difference.

   Thank you for reviewing this query.

Regards,
Carolyn Tomlin

Check the following:

- I've worked with this editor before, so I used his first name.

- Title stated first. Also, use title in subject line of email.

- Grab the editor's attention with a strong hook. (Data stated and source)

- Indicate how I plan to develop the article. (Interviews, medical profession, parents, social worker)

- Mention an article/photo package.

- Why is the topic important to the writer?

- End with a direct request to write the article. (suggest word count) Thank the editor for reviewing.

- Keep the query letter to one page. (Sometimes a query requires more space. Rules are made to be broken.)

Based on this query, do you think the editor will respond?

EXAMPLE OF A BAD MAGAZINE QUERY

Dear Editor,

I've like to write the best article you'll ever publish. My writing credits include writing community news for my local paper and working on the high school yearbook. In fact, years ago my English teacher once told me I should be a writer. I guess I've been writing all my life.

Although your magazine may not be the tops, I'm willing to send you my articles, anyway. You need articles, and I really need to make some cash. Never fret, I won't charge you very much! (Ha-ha.)

If you'll give me names of people to interview, I'll get right on to it. I'll write and re-write until I get it perfect for your magazine.

Please respond soon, as I've sent out this same letter to dozens of other magazines. I'm sure I'll have more work than I can possibly produce.

See you later,
Your best friend,
I'm-A-Writer

Check the following:

- Identify the correct editor. This is like a hole in the water. By sending an email to a general mailbox, the editor may never see this query.

- Writing community news for the local paper and school yearbook are not impressive to most editors. If you don't have published clips, mention volunteer work and life experiences. Don't tell them what you don't have.

- Never insult the editor of a publication as one of low pay.

- Avoid cuteness as to an honorarium.

- Writers should pitch their own subjects or topics for articles. Don't depend on editors to supply you with interviews or leads. However, once you become a regular writer for their magazine, the editor may give assignments focusing on topics or themes.

Do you believe editors will be sending him work?

RULES FOR ONLINE WRITING QUERIES

Most free-lance writers know the rules in writing the traditional query letter. But are there differences between publishing with hardcopy magazines and publishing with online publications? Some standard rules apply; but there are others you need to know. Here are the basic guidelines?

Rule #1. Be professional. Always use a professional tone as used in a business letter. Use the proper address; include paragraphs, complete sentences and a proper closing. Avoid slang or cuteness. Unless...the magazine follows this format.

Rule #2. Use links for extras. A query for an online magazine can include links to published clips, writer's bio and resume´ if they are available online. Many editors appreciate these links instead of long emails. If they're interested in you as a writer, or your idea, they can click on the link for more information.

Rule #3. Avoid attachments unless requested. Viruses can be picked up from attachments and create loss of data from an editor's computer. Also, your software may be different from the editor's program. Send the query in the body of the email and also as an attachment. The editor has the option of choosing either. Mention additional information available on your website. Or, send additional material upon request as an attachment.

Rule #4. Don't worry the editor! Check the guidelines in the Writer's Market for the range of "wait" time. If you haven't heard within this period, email that you are checking the status of your online query. Send the same query a second time as a reminder, along with a brief message.

When I haven't heard from an editor and the range of time has expired, I email or call. I've had these responses: "Sorry, but I've lost your article. Could you resend?" "My computer crashed about the time you submitted your manuscript." "Our committee hasn't made a decision, yet." And often, these follow-up contacts results in a contract. Never be afraid to check again. Always be courteous and willing to make changes if needed. You could end up being a part of the editor's stable of writers they pull in for extra assignments.

Success for writing queries in both traditional magazines and online magazines depend on knowing the magazine, identifying the audience and treating the editor with a sense of professionalism. Simplify the editor's job and you increase your chances of being published.

WRITING THE LETTER OF INTRODUCTION

Instead of the query letter, use a Letter of Introduction (LOI) for trade journals and custom publications. How can you convince an editor you are the person they want to work with? What makes you unique?

As most magazines are now online, I scan two or three articles in the archives. Reading the Editor's Column, you discover a special interest or focus of the editor. I noticed an editor's column that she recently adopted 2 shelter dogs. This was an opening to respond to her front-of-the-book article and mention, that I, too, have a shelter dog. Pick up on this and make a positive comment. Or, perhaps you read an article that is interesting or helpful. Make a response. Look at the following example of a brief LOI:

Good Example of a Letter of Introduction

> Subject: Pro freelance writer available
>
> Hi (Editor's name),
>
> Thanks for sharing your thoughts in the editor's column on _____. I've had the same experience myself (or something to relate to the article).
>
> My name is Carolyn Tomlin and I'm a professional freelance writer. I noticed your magazine is expanding to audiences in Central America and I wanted to contact you for freelance work. I've traveled to many of these countries and islands and taught basic Spanish to students. I've published over 4,000 magazine articles and teach writing-to-publish workshops. May I send you some published clips?
>
> Please reply to this email if you're interested. Thanks!
>
> Carolyn Tomlin

Check for the following:

- Correct editor's name was used
- By reading her column, she was aware I was familiar with the magazine.
- I show a connection with the area and language.
- The email shows I'm a published writer and teacher.
- The editor is under no obligation to respond. However, most editors will suggest you email published clips.
- It's brief and to the point.

What are the chances the writer receives a response?

Bad Example of a LOI

> Hi there!
> I just read your Editor's Column and I must say, "I disagree with you! Surely, you don't believe that stuff! By the way, do you need someone to "really write" what people want to read? I can do almost anything on any subject—just name it! I guess you would say I'm a published writer as I write our church newsletter that goes out to 200 people each week. My writing background includes an online course, and that's about it.
> Would love to send you lots of articles—if you're interested. Forget the snail mail route—I'm up-to-date with the latest computer programs!!! Thanks a bunch!
> Wanna-Be-a-Writer

Check for the following:

- Did not use editor's name.
- Made negative comments about editor's column.
- Suggested he could write much better.
- No experience writing-to-publish
- Editors don't want "lots of articles." They want well researched and written queries.
- Boasting about technical ability.
- Improper signature.

Do you think this editor will respond?

Q.1. What is one mistake writers make when writing a query?

A.1. Not addressing the query to the correct editor—never send email to a general mailbox, such as editor@magazine.com. Chances are a secretary reads the email and makes a decision on those sent to the editor. (See additional information in Session 1, "Know Your Magazine.")

Q.2. Is a catchy title important in a query?

A.2. A title helps the editor visualize the placement and how the article will appear in the magazine. Don't make your title too broad, or too narrow. Know the magazine as to type of titles used. Do they use a number, such as: "5 Ways to Remove a Stain" or include the words: New, Surprise, or Amazing in the title? Such as: "Seven Amazing Exercises to Tone Your Legs."

Q.3. When writing a query letter, how can a writer catch the editor's attention quickly?

A.3. Hopefully, the editor will think "Wow" instead of a rubber stamp of "No" or worse, hitting the delete button. Instead of telling the editor of your background, list of publishing credit, how you just "love" their magazine—write just the facts, Madam! Just the facts! How does the magazine you are querying begin articles? Do they use an anecdote, data, statistics, or quote from an expert? Start off your query with a lead that editors can't resist and they'll read to the end. If you're writing an article that includes personal experience—start in the middle. Then, go back and explain how you plan to write the article.

Section 5

OUTLINING AND SUBMITTING YOUR ARTICLE

"A man's character may be learned from the adjectives which he habitually

uses in conversation."

~ Mark Twain

When writing an article, begin with a plan—or an outline. Who will you interview? Did you find current data on the topic? Will you use sidebars? Bullets? Is your article in a similar format as those in the magazine?

When is it time to let it go and hit "Send"? When is it time to either fish— or cut bait?

WHY OUTLINE?

Would you begin to build a house without a blueprint? Or, plan a college curriculum without some sort of guide? On a much smaller scale, it's the same with writing an article. Start with an outline. Writers ask: When do you decide on an outline? This works for me: I work best when focusing on one topic at a time. Perhaps, under pressure, you focus well on several topics.

It's what works for you. A friend says, "There's no one right way to do everything." Maybe I'm fortunate in being able to write fast and complete several original articles each week. Decide what you are comfortable with and follow through.

Outline during routine work when your mind doesn't have to "think" about what you're doing. For example: pulling weeds in the flower garden, walking the dog, washing dishes, and yes, even sitting through a boring conference. A warm body may have to be in the chair, but they can't capture your mind. Always have a piece of paper, and a pen handy—just in case. Of course, I've used a paper napkin when in a tight! Then, when I move to the computer most of my work is complete. You've pulled in your sources for interviews, data, and quotes. I can write fast, edit an edit some more.

Also, do a task analysis. When faced with a difficult job, break it down into smaller parts. Small jobs are easier handled than larger ones.

If taking a walk, I use my Smartphone to record my outline. Refrain from using any phone or mobile device when driving as you must focus on your own driving as well as the approaching driver.

USE THE CREATIVE PROCESS IN DEVELOPING THE ARTICLE

Going back to days as a faculty member at Union University in Jackson, TN, I taught education students to use the Creative Process when faced with a new task. Although this is an old approach, it still works today.

1. **Preparation** – Involves the necessary background of experiences to do the work.

2. **Incubation** – The stage not visible, but the individual appears to be thinking about anything, but the problem.

3. **Illumination** – This stage is when that moment of insight or a spark lights up and a solution is found.

4. **Verification** – The final stage is when a "hunch" is subjected to testing and refinement. (G. Wallas, *The Art of Thought* (New York: Harcourt Brace, 1926).

SUGGESTIONS FOR FINDING INTERVIEW SOURCES

One area that new writers experience problems with is finding expert sources for interviews. Instead of your mother, cousin, your best friend and the grocer, who can you contact? Editors do not want these people. It's unacceptable. Instead, who makes a good resource?

Tracking these people down is like looking for a needle in a haystack, but it's necessary. Think about these sources for good interviews:

1. College and university faculty, especially if known as a center for research.

2. Foundation presidents. If possible, start with the person at the top.

3. CEO of major companies and businesses.

4. Authors who have written a best-selling book or those known for a specific genre. Also, check "new" books that are coming out.

5. State and U.S. government agencies. Check the latest census report and the Centers for Disease Control (CDC).

6. Social media. Throw out a request to your contacts on Facebook, LinkedIn and Twitter. You can even ask these contacts to forward the request to their contacts.

7. Other sources include: Help a Reporter Out. (www.helpareporter.com) and ProNet (www.prnewswire.com/profnet/)

Don't hesitate to make these connections. Professional people need writers to keep their name or projects in the news.

HOW DO I APPROACH A SOURCE?

After tracking down an email or a business phone number, I call and say something like, "I'm working on an article for XYX magazine. Will you give me a quote on (your recent book, a new trend in your sales department, or whatever)?

Get a strong quote that can be used to "Wow" the editor in the query. Then, I say, "May I get back to you if this query is accepted for a 10 to 15 minutes phone conversation?"

If at all possible, I prefer to use a phone instead of email. It's fresher and I feel the personality coming through. Do your research and know something about the person, business, etc. before the call. Write a list of questions to help keep the dialogue on track. I ask permission to record the talk, put the phone on speaker which frees my hands, and type the answers. Being a fast typist helps!

GET OVER THE PROCRASTINATING STAGE AND WRITE!

Most of the time, writing is fun. I'm excited about starting a new article. But let's face it—some days I just can't get it done! This usually happens when I'm away from the writing process for several days. For example: Spending two weeks in Russia, I shot photographs and took notes for a multitude of articles. Thinking...when I return home, I'll write non-stop, day and night. But after my two week hiatus, I couldn't get back to writing.

Assignments and deadlines crept closer. Editors called. Emails popped up. After having a good talk with myself, I knew what I had to do. Put my bottom in the chair and start writing. Could I write 20 minutes at a time—without leaving the computer? Could I promise myself a "treat" like a cup of tea, after I wrote 300 words? Well, somehow this approach worked.

Also, I set my Smartphone to call me every 20 minutes—just to see that I was writing.

Another way I got back into the groove was to change my attitude. Did I want to give up what had taken me years to learn? Or, to have editors forget my name? It can happen—and fast! I had to remind myself that writing was a wonderful part of my life and I was fortunate to have this passion.

So, the next time you start to procrastinate on an article—or writing in general—don't put off until the last minute to write that article. You'll end the day feeling you accomplished something and can move on to other areas of writing you enjoy!

WHAT'S THE FUSS ABOUT WORD COUNT?

Editors have a limited amount of space in a magazine. Regular columns and departments use the same pages monthly. If your assignment is for 500 words and you send in 400—not good! Or, if you send in 700—not good, either. One editor I work with advises to not go over 10 percent. It's better to go over a little, than under. This way the editor doesn't have to find additional information to fill in the gaps.

Linda Formichelli, editor of *Write Your Way Out of the Rat Race…And Step Into a Career You Love* (Kindle, PDF and audio) offers this advice:

1. **Turn the extra info into a sidebar** and pretend like I'm being the most generous writer on earth by offering an optional sidebar for free.

2. **Highlight the info I think is the best candidate to be cut** and tell the editor, "I really wanted to include this but it puts the article way over word count. If you need to cut it down, this is the info I suggest you cut." Sometimes, the editor does decide to leave in that copy. But if she really needs to make words count, I've made it easier for her.

3. **Ask the editor if I can have more space** to include the information I feel is important. (Sometimes they say yes!)

COMMUNICATING WITH YOUR EDITOR

There is still a bit of work to do, before you submit the assigned article. Communicate with your editor and check off these areas.

1. Write a brief cover letter as part of your email to accompany your article. Thank the editor for this opportunity to contribute to their publication.

2. This letter reduces the number of questions—before they're asked. I explain that my tone matched the style of the magazine, the gender, and age group of their readers.

3. Close by saying that you look forward to working with this magazine again.

4. Paste the article into the body of the email message and also include it as an attachment.

5. Send yourself a blind copy (BBC).

6. Update your records to show the name of the magazine, the article title, and the date emailed. Keep records current.

THE POWER OF PHOTOS

It's been said, "A picture is worth a thousand words!" I agree and would add: It can mean the difference between a query being accepted and, ending in the slush pile.

With digital photography, there's no excuse not to learn the mechanics of a camera. I would say 75 percent of my queries include two or three digitals that support the proposed article. By reviewing the query, plus digitals, the editor can envision how the layout will look in his magazine. Your photos may not be used, but the editor has an idea of how the article will appear. And the reason for this number not being 100 percent—some of the magazines do not use photographs. Others use a graphic designer on staff.

Check the *Writer's Market* or online guidelines about payment. Some publications pay separately for photos and payment is made when the article is published—even though you received payment for the manuscript when accepted. Other magazines consider an article/photo package and the writer is "highly encouraged" to supply photos. No extra payment is given for this contract. If you can supply photos, this puts you ahead of the mob of writers that want this assignment.

Unless you have a professional photographer who goes with you, travel writers must master using a camera and produce saleable photos. For example, say you plan to write an article on China's Terra-Cotta Warriors. It's highly unlikely a magazine would pay the expenses of a photographer to travel to China to make these shots. When I can not make quality photos while on location, I contact a tourism bureau or convention center to supply these. However, there's no pay and you must provide the owner's name. Another source is www.googleimages.com for non-copyrighted photos. If a photo is made by a government agency, you have the right to use this image at no cost to you. After all, our taxes pay the photographer's salary. You must list the source and can not accept payment. My advice: Make your own quality photos. Easier than tracking down a photo! And usually, with pay!

Generic Royalty-free, Public Domain Photos

- http://www.ars.usda.gov/is/graphics/photos

- http://photogallery.ncrs.usa.gov/index.asp (find photos by states)

- http://www.usda.gv/oc/photo/opclibra.thm

- www.istockphoto.com (charges a small fee)

- www.picasa.com (Free software download to store, organize and email digitals. I recommend this simple to use software to transfer photos from your digital camera to your computer.)

Ansel Adams, the famous photographer once said, "Photography is more than a medium for factual communication of ideas. It is a creative art."

SUBMITTING YOUR ARTICLE

Life changes! When I first started writing, I typed my article on a word-processor, made a copy, took it to the Post Office to be weighed, purchase stamps, included a SASE with stamps for return of the entire manuscript—just in case it was rejected. Oh yes, I also sent a floppy disk. Sending slides or printed photos was really a headache. I spent lots of hard-earned money to make duplicates, place them in a protected envelope, purchased insurance , wrote on the outside of the package—Do Not Bend-Photos, Included.

With electronic submission, editors now expect emails as the preferred method of delivery. In the subject line, I write: Tomlin, name of article (or query), date. If the article is scheduled for a certain month, I add this date. Because attachments may transfer a virus to an editor's computer, I copy and paste the article into the body of the email as well as send an attachment. This gives the editor a choice on opening the article.

Make certain your email went through by checking your "Sent" box.

KEEPING GOOD RECORDS

If you're like me, it's difficult to remember what I wrote yesterday, last week, and especially last year! That's why keeping good records is essential to your writing career. On my favorite computer, I have a record of every article published since 1994. Last count, I had 48 single-spaced pages. Each year I start over in numbering the submissions. Under each month I list the magazine, article title, editor's name, date emailed and if photos were submitted. If the article was published, I list the honorarium, and the date the check arrived. This simple method works for me. I can pull up the file and see when an article was published, search for an editor's name and if it was used as a reprint. **Important:** Make a backup file on a jump drive or CD. This is one file you can't afford to lose.

FILING YOUR PUBLISHED CLIPS

After an article is published, writers are sent a copy (sometimes 3 copies) of the magazine. To keep these organized, I remove the article (carefully) and place in a plastic sleeve and insert in a 3-ring binder notebook. For magazines where I've written a column for several years, I have a separate notebook for this publication. The same goes for newspaper columns. Others are listed: Secular Market, Vol. I and II; Christian Market, Vol. I and II. Each notebook contains tabs listed in alphabetical order. When these fill to capacity, I'll add Vol. III. Shelved in a large bookcase, I can easily pull any article in minutes.

This is no easy task with publishing between 200-250 articles each year. As each magazine arrives with a published article, I immediately remove that one and place in a basket. In time (sometimes a year, or more), I devote a day or so to inserting each article in a plastic sleeve and placing in the 3-ring binder. What a relief to mark this chore off my "to-do" list!

I think each writer has to develop a filing system that works. You may try several before you are satisfied with your chosen method.

QUESTIONS FROM WRITERS—ANSWERS YOU NEED

Q-1. What is a sure-fire way to organize an article?

A-1. That depends. It depends on the format used in the magazine you query. This old standard has served me for many articles. Begin with a strong hook, data, who says this is important, point 1, point 2, point 3 (points contain your resources and interviews) and a conclusion that returns to the hook in some way.

Q-2. How can I make certain the data and research are correct?

A-2. Instead of pulling from a newspaper or another magazine article, go to the original source. Confirm your information from a reliable organization or foundation.

Q-3. An editor I'm working with suggested I use the "Inverted Pyramid" style for this article. Can you explain it briefly?

A-3. The Inverted Pyramid is often taught in journalism classes. Like newspaper reporting, it describes who, what, when, where and why in the opening paragraph. The reader has the basic information and does not have to read the entire article. General information comes in later or last.

Section 6

WAITING FOR THE CONTRACT …AND CHECK IN THE MAIL

"Success is not final, failure is not fatal; it is the courage to continue that counts."

~ Winston Churchill

Hopefully, you'll receive a contract detailing the word count, deadline, rights offered and payment. But what if the article query is rejected? This section offers advice on your next step and how to place the article with another publisher.

NEGOTIATING WITH EDITORS

Whether it's the first contract—or the hundredth, most writers are excited about selling an article. But before you yell, "YES" think about the terms of the contact. Take time to consider these questions before you sign on the dotted line.

1. What is the honorarium?

Department and column articles may be set in stone. It's a "take- it-or-leave it" job. However, there are times you can negotiate. If an editor offers you a rate below what you were expecting, ask for more. Offer a reason why the fee should be higher. Say, "This article required several interviews plus other follow-up work. I usually received about $500 for an article like this. Could you increase your offer?"

The bottom line...the editor may say "No." Will you accept this offer or walk? It's up to you. However, he may say "Yes," or "I'll see what I can do."

2. What is the deadline?

Writers who consider this their full-time business may be inclined to accept too many assignments. It has happen to me. Check your calendar. Do you have other large assignments due the same week? Are you planning a vacation or a family reunion? If you feel this would put you in a rush, request more time. You might say, "This article will require four interviews, plus several hours of research. In order to do my best work, I'll need a few extra days. Is this possible?" Let the editor know in advance; not the day it's due. The few times I've asked for a bit of extra time, it was granted. However, I've billed myself as a writer who has never missed a deadline. The bottom line is: don't accept too many deadlines close together.

3. What is the Word Count?

What if your query suggests a 2,000-word feature article and the editor ask for 500 words? Negotiate. You might say, "I wanted to interview 4 teens who received a high score on the ACT Test and tips for making this happen. Would it be possible to expand this to a 1,000-word article?

Here again, give a reason to backup your request. Know the magazine and suggest the article be placed in a department piece instead of a feature.

4. What Rights Are Offered?

Yes, I've written for "all rights" but I try to avoid this when possible. The publication owns the article! Fact. I prefer to sell First North American Serial Rights, which allows me to use the article as a reprint. Some magazines have in their contract that you can not submit it to another editor for three months; others six months. Non-exclusive perpetual license allows the writer to publish the article but the publisher still owns the rights to use it in other places.

Online rights are usually combined with the contract, as most magazines have their publication on the Internet.

5. When Will You Be Paid?

This information usually is included in the *Writer's Market.* Some pay on acceptance; others on publication; and others three to six months after publication.

Consider this: What if the magazine pays on publication and your article keeps getting pushed back? Or, the magazine folds and you're yet to be published? Some editors won't change their policy, but you can request that you "will" be paid on a certain date, regardless if published or not. Have this stated in the contact you sign.

Serious writers know how to negotiate when working with a contract. If you aren't satisfied with a magazine, there are plenty of others that need your work. Keep several queries going out on a regular basis so you can choose the editors where you want to publish. You may need to turn down some articles, in order to write for those better markets.

Hopefully, you'll receive a contract detailing the word count, deadline, rights offered and payment. But what if the article is rejected? This section offers advice on your next step and how to place the article with another publisher.

REASONS ARTICLES ARE REJECTED

Realize that a rejection letter is nothing personal. The editor doesn't know you! Look at some of the reasons this happens:

1. The editor hasn't had his morning coffee.
2. Its late afternoon and her eyes are very tired when she opens your file.
3. They ran a similar topic a year ago.

4. There is an article in the pipeline that will be out in 2 months. (Writers do not know this unless the editor shares this information.)

5. Your article is based on "new" information. By the time it is published, perhaps 6 – 9 months, the material will be old.

6. You're an unknown and you queried for a feature article. The editor is really taking a chance by offering an "unknown" a feature story. In fact, her job could be on the line. Start with a department column or smaller article—usually located in the front of the magazine.

7. The editor who assigned your article is no longer on the staff. The new editor doesn't know you. (Sometimes when a new editor comes onboard all files of previous articles on hold, are discarded. It's happen to me several times!).

8. Keep as many articles and queries out as you can handle. When this happens—what's one rejection letter? The old adage of "Don't put all your eggs in one basket still holds true!"

George Washington Carver said, "Ninety-nine percent of the failures come from people who have the habit of making excuses."

WHAT YOU CAN DO—WHILE WAITING

Hours turn into days, days into weeks and often weeks become months. And you still haven't heard from that article you research, interviewed and spent blood, sweat and tears to produce your best work. What should you do? Check the *Writer's Market* for the time range as to a response. If the time has passed, email the editor, identify yourself and say, "I'm checking the status of (name of article) submitted on (date). They may ask you to wait while they check, or they may get back to you. Always be courteous and professional. In this situation, it's the editor's call.

A writer friend holds the world's record on having a magazine hold an article. Twenty-five years ago, she submitted an article to a German magazine. Last month, she received a letter and a small check that the manuscript had been published!

Sometimes articles become lost in email, they may end up in the wrong mailbox, or sometimes a committee makes the decision. Be patient, yet assertive. How you handle this situation could depend on being called on again for an assignment.

Keep Those Queries Moving

For years, I tried to keep, on the average 25 queries out at all times. I still keep several out, but not 25. When you know the magazine and know the audience, your rejections drop and the acceptance letters come in. As you collect more published clips and establish yourself with several magazines, editors come to you. That's not to say you shouldn't always be searching for new markets. Part of the challenge of writing is working with new people.

Go to Plan B

Look at this scenario: You wrote a query, which was accepted. A month later, you email an article that required research, interviews, numerous emails and phone calls. Three months later, you receive a letter that states:

Dear Writer,

We (meaning the editors) appreciate (when you've read this far—you know, the article is being rejected) you allowing us to review your article. As it does not meet our present needs, we encourage you to submit it to another publication. Unfortunately, we do not offer a kill fee for unaccepted articles. When you have another idea, we would be happy to review the query.

Sincerely,
The Editors

This is a form letter sent for all rejected articles! So what do you do? Hold your head high, chin up, and move to Plan B. It's not the end of the world! What's the worse thing that could happen? Think of this as a learning experience and try the second magazine on your list. This happens to all writers at one time of another. My advice: Write a brief email to the editor thanking them for reviewing your article and that you will send another idea in a few days.

Now, go back over the article. Where could you improve? Do you have the right quotes from good sources? One writer suggested one quote, plus one, for every 500-words. For a 2,000 word article, she used 4 quotes, plus one. Did you find typos? Have someone with good writing skills review the article. If the editor has made any suggestions, think of these as a positive response. Apply them to the next query and article.

KEEPING A BALANCE IN YOUR LIFE

Perhaps this "wait" time for a contract to arrive is a good place to look at what you do with the times you aren't writing—the times when you're with family and friends. Writers often ask how I've been able to publish over 4,000 magazine articles and still have a life? The secret is keeping a balance in everything you do. It's not always easy, but the alternative is even worse.

Like you, I too, wear many hats. I'm a wife, mother, grandmother, friend, teacher and writer. Often I ask myself: which of these are more important in my life? If I had to give one up, which one could I do without? Some are not optional—some are a given! This is a question you must answer for yourself. But for me, I'll keep them all.

Also, learn how to write fast, decrease the time you spend researching, interviewing, and editing so you actually spend less time on this process. I urge you to keep a record of the number of hours you spend on each article. Will you be surprised? Whittle it down and reduce the time involved. Some students, who attend my Magazine Writing Workshops, have shared they have been working on "one" article for months!

QUESTIONS FROM WRITERS—ANSWERS YOU NEED

Q-1. I wrote an article for a national magazine about a man in Tennessee who trains therapy dogs. The article was rejected. Any suggestions for placing the article elsewhere?

A- 1 Although the topic was interesting, broaden your area. If this was a national magazine, move out of one state and find several sources in other places. Otherwise, look for a regional or state magazine.

Q- 2. I plan to query a woman's health magazine that focuses on nutrition. Although I'm aware of healthy eating habits, I'm not an expert, nor do I have a degree in this field. Suggestions, please?

A-2. Use anecdotes, quotes, and research to build your query, then expand the article. It isn't necessary that you are an authority on nutrition—that's why you need the experts in this field!

Q-3. I've written a monthly column for one magazine for a couple of years. Every month I received a check. It's been three months and I've haven't been paid. Should I contact the editor?

A-3. Of course. Editors turn in a request for payment and another department handles this area. Due to human error, sometimes a breakdown occurs. Once this happen to me and it took about three months to have it corrected. By all means, contact the editor.

Resources

I encourage, you the writer, to sign up for these excellent online free tutorials. You'll receive weekly tips for writing for the magazine market. Occasionally, these writers offer inexpensive online workshops that are worth their weight in gold. Some of the information in this book is adapted from these sources.

- Linda Formichelli, http://www.therenegadewriter.com

- Carol Tice, http://www.makealivingwriting.com

Appendices

TIPS FOR BOOSTING YOUR WRITING CAREER IN 10 MINUTES OR LESS

I believe that small things make a difference! And, small things often pay big dividends. It's true of writing! Taking a few minutes can help you reach your goals and make you more productive when you write. For example:

- When using the phone, walk your house. Simple exercise clears the mind and you're able to focus.

- Close each work day with a clean and clutter-free desk. You'll look forward to beginning a new project or completing an assignment the following morning.

- Write a handwritten "thank-you" note to an editor who accepted your article.

- Sip a cup of herbal tea.

- Line up people for interviews and set a time to talk.

- Identify and save websites for data and research. Keep a list of areas where you need a resource person. This saves time when working on a deadline.

- Read books, just for fun, for 10 minutes a day.

- Add to your list of quotations.

- Spend a few minutes listening—really listening to someone.

- Organize your files. Delete those you'll never use again.

- Before bedtime, make a "to-do" list for the next day. About writing, of course!

- Take a day—or a week—off without feeling guilty. Book a tour. Make reservations at a favorite restaurant. Plan a family reunion.

It's amazing what you can accomplish in 10 minutes when you're focused. Time away from work recharges the mind and body.

Also by Carolyn Tomlin

The following books, in hardcopy, paperback, and as ebooks, can be ordered and/or downloaded through amazon.com as well as other outlets.

 **Boot Camp for Christian Writers Carolyn Tomlin Writing-To-Publish: The Basic Foundations (Volume 2)**
Includes: "The Publishing Opportunities That Await You"
"How to Find Great Ideas to Write About"

 **The Basics of Article Publishing for Print Magazines & Online Magazines: Boot Camp for Christian Writers (Volume 4)**
Includes: "Getting Started in the Magazine Market"
"The Magazine Market—Tools of the Trade"
"How to Identify Your Audience"
"Knowing the Magazine"

 **Four More Articles Editors Love and How to Write Them: Boot Camp for Christian Writers (Volume 6)**
Includes: "Writing and Selling the How-to Article"
"Finding Markets for Newspaper and Mini-Columns"
"Breaking into Magazine Markets with Fillers"
"Seeing the World—Writing the Travel Article"

 ***More Secrets to Getting Published—Again and Again and Again! (Vol 8)***
Includes: "Photography: Creating the Perfect Article Package"
"One Idea—Multiple Markets"
"Networking Successfully with Magazine Editors"

 **Writing Grants for Faith-Based Organizations and Community Non-Profits (Vol 10)** Includes: "Identifying Sources for Grants"
"Key Areas of the Application"
"Tips for Being Funded"
"Selecting a Grant-Writing Committee"

What I Wish I'd Known Sooner: Parents

Do you ever wish the things about being a parent hadn't taken you so long to learn? This book is part of a series and focuses on the joys of being a parent. Bits of wisdom the author learned from raising two children are interwoven with prayers. You'll laugh, and rejoice in this role of "Parenthood." Section two, The Home and School Connection, offers guidance and self-help for parents as they deal with school-related issues. You'll find answers to Bus Safety, Making Friends, Peer Pressure, How to Talk with the Teacher, and other topics.

What I Wish I'd Known Sooner: Teachers

Part of a series, this book is written for educators. Included are bits of wisdom, prayers for teachers and students. Chapters are divided into areas affecting teachers, such as First Day of School, Open House, Bus Duty, and others. This series has been used in speaking to teacher groups, given as a gift and as a quick read for those who are able to laugh instead of cry when facing situations that arise in everyday life. Prayers give the reader strength and courage.

More Alike than Different (story and coloring book)

By Carolyn Tomlin, illustrated by Ellen C. Maze

This is a story of Matthew, a young boy, who makes friends with children in his community from different cultures and ethnic groups. He soon learns that God made and loves all children and that we are all "more alike than different." Black and white line drawings provide a kinesthetic form of learning as children color the simple pictures.

The Secret Holocaust Diaries: The Untold Story of Nonna Bannister by Nonna Bannister, Carolyn Tomlin and Denise George

Nonna Bannister almost carried a secret to her Tennessee grave. As the only known family survivor of the Holocaust, she came to America after the World War II, married Henry Bannister and did not tell him about being a Holocaust survivor for over forty years. Hidden under her dress, her grandmother tied a little ticking pillow filled with family photos. In this pillow, Nonna kept her secret. It's a true story of a little Russian girl who survived because of faith in God, love of family and the ability to forgive her enemies. This award-winning book was Published by *Tyndale House Publishers*.

The following books are out-of-print but may be available on <u>www.half.com</u>, <u>www.amazon.com</u> or other outlets.

Teachers as Published Writers

A practical guide to writing and publishing for teachers. Readers will learn how to know the magazine market, understand the reader's needs and sell ideas developed in the classroom. Other teachers will benefit from your ideas across the curriculum. Published by *Judy Wood Publishing Company.*

From the Cat's Point of View

Written for cat lovers, this book gives a glimpse inside the mind of our furry friends. Can cats read your mind? Do they relate to your emotions? Read looking at life through the eyes of a cat to discover more about yourself—as well as that of your feline.
Published by *Judy Wood Publishing Company.*

More Alike than Different, (A children's story book)

Focusing on accepting multicultural differences, Matthew, a young boy meets the people in his neighborhood. Written as an easy-reader and as a listen-to-me book, children will soon be repeating the phrases uses over and over again. Published by *WMU Publishers.*

Mental Pause

Taking a humorous approach at menopause, the author describes emotions and behaviors related to this time in a woman's life. Published by *Judy Wood Publishing Company.*

True Tales or Tall Tales: You Decide with Denise George and Carolyn Tomlin

Some stories are just too strange to be true—or are they? Based on stories from the news and the writer's creativity, you will not know if this is a true story or a tall tale. Turn to the back of the book to find the answer. Written for upper elementary and middle school students. Published by *Judy Wood Publishing Company.*

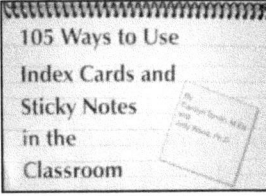

105 Ways to Use Index Cards and Sticky Notes in the Classroom, Judy Wood and Carolyn Tomlin

This book offers suggestions for using index cards and sticky notes in all areas of the curriculum—from reading, math, science, social studies and others. Published by *Judy Wood Publishing Company.*

A Parent's Guide to Summer Survival

School's out! The long-awaited summer vacation has finally arrived. For most kids, it's approximately 10 weeks (or 70 days, or 1,680 hours) each summer. For students, nothing could be better. For parents, what will you do with the kids all day? Instead of fussing, being bored, or having a "panic attack" try some of the great ideas in this book. Published by *Judy Wood Publishing Company.*

365 Email Messages for Students and Teachers (with Veronica Coulston)

Make using the Internet and Email fun for students! Teachers find questions from the curriculum based on history, fine arts, sports, literature, social studies, science and other topics. Each day they email their class a question. The student must find the answer by using the Internet. Or, students can post the question for their peers. This is a fun way to learn, as well as master using the Internet and email. Published by *Judy Wood Publishing Company.*

The Tutor's Handbook: Math (Grade 2)

This helpful guide offers enrichment for students and includes: a sample tutoring session, creative tutoring strategies, reproducible work sheets and real-life math connections. Published by *Frank Schaffer Publications.*

First Steps in Missions, Vol. 6 with Tammie Worsham

Activities and ideas for Mission Friends and Teachers. This book offers fun and learning-based activities for home-schoolers, Vacation Bible Clubs, Christian schools and others.
Published by Woman's Missionary Union

About the Author

Carolyn Tomlin has been writing and publishing since 1988. She has authored 19 books and over 4,000 published articles in magazines such as *Entrepreneur, Kansas City News, American Profile, Tennessee Home & Farm, Home Life, Mature Living, ParentLife*, and many others. She and Denise George have written 14 books for the popular seminar, Boot Camp for Christian Writers. She is the co-author of the award-winning book, *The Secret Holocaust Diaries: The Untold Story of Nonna Bannister.* The book is in the 13th printing and has been translated into 6 languages. Her latest books are *What I Wish I'd Known Sooner: Parents, What I Wish I'd Known Sooner: Teachers* and *More Alike Than Different* (a story and coloring book for children.). Carolyn is married to Dr. Matt Tomlin, a Southern Baptist minister. They have two adult children, Cindy Tomlin Coulston and Kevin Tomlin, and six grandchildren.

You may contact Carolyn Tomlin at:
Carolyn's email address: tomlinm@bellsouth.net
Web Page: www.carolyntomlin.com
Boot Camp for Christian Writers- Beeson's website:
http://www.beesondivinity.com/bootcampforchristianwriters
Connect with Carolyn Tomlin on Facebook or LinkedIn.

Seminar Notes

www.ingramcontent.com/pod-product-compliance
Lightning Source LLC
Chambersburg PA
CBHW080518290526
45790CB00006B/2219